I0796594
To..
From..

TO HIM WHO SPREAD OUT THE EARTH ABOVE THE WATERS, FOR HIS LOVING KINDNESS ENDURES FOREVER.
Psalms 136:6

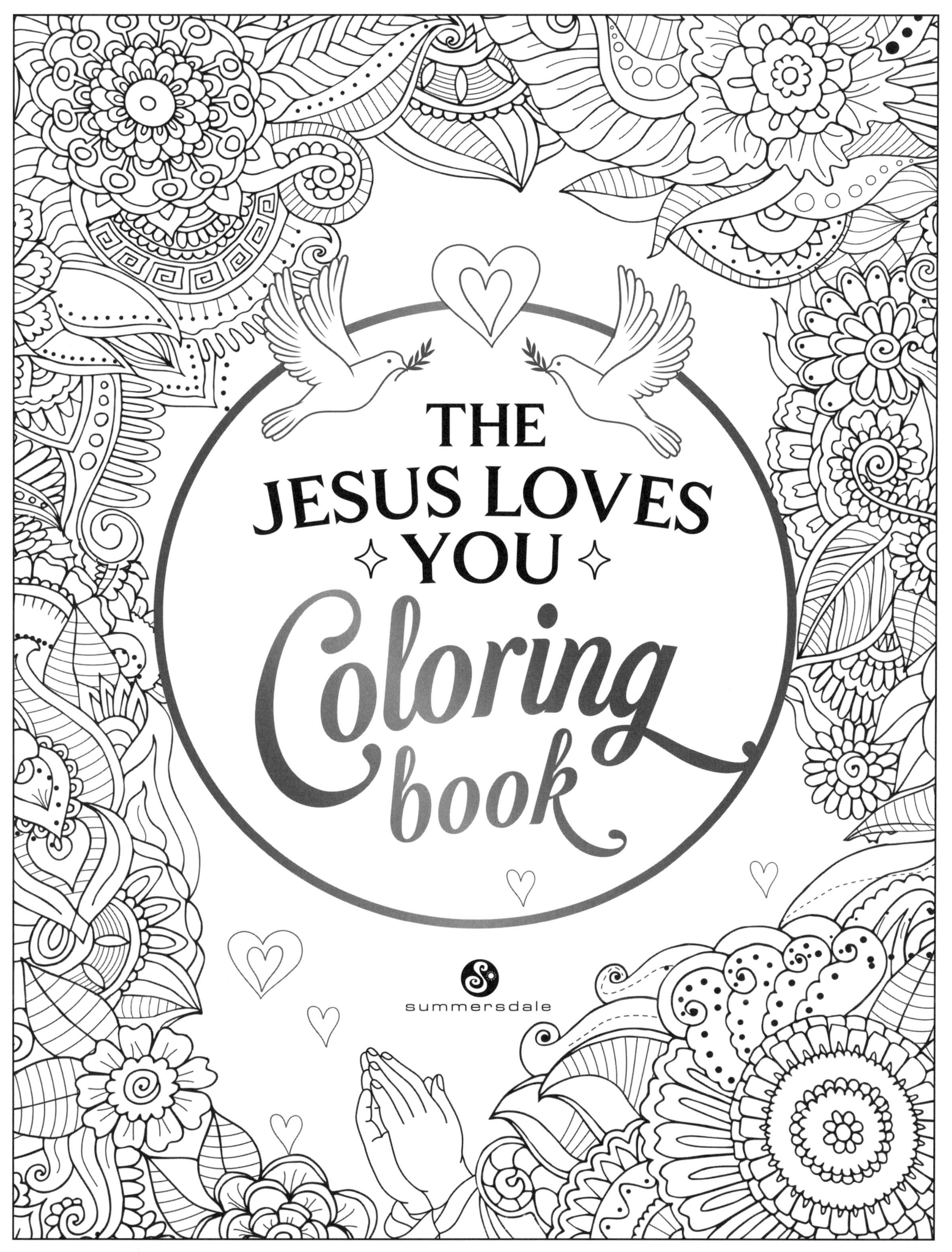
THE
JESUS LOVES
YOU
Coloring
book
summersdale

THE JESUS LOVES YOU COLORING BOOK

Compiled by Alice Billing and Abi Reeves

All Bible verses taken from the World English Bible.

An Hachette UK Company
www.hachette.co.uk

Summersdale Publishers
Part of Octopus Publishing Group Limited
Carmelite House
50 Victoria Embankment
LONDON
EC4Y 0DZ
UK

This FSC® label means that materials used for the product have been responsibly sourced

www.summersdale.com

The authorized representative in the EEA is Hachette Ireland, 8 Castlecourt Centre, Dublin 15, D15 XTP3, Ireland (email: info@hbgi.ie)

Printed and bound in China

ISBN: 978-1-83799-616-2

Pray
MORE
Worry
LESS

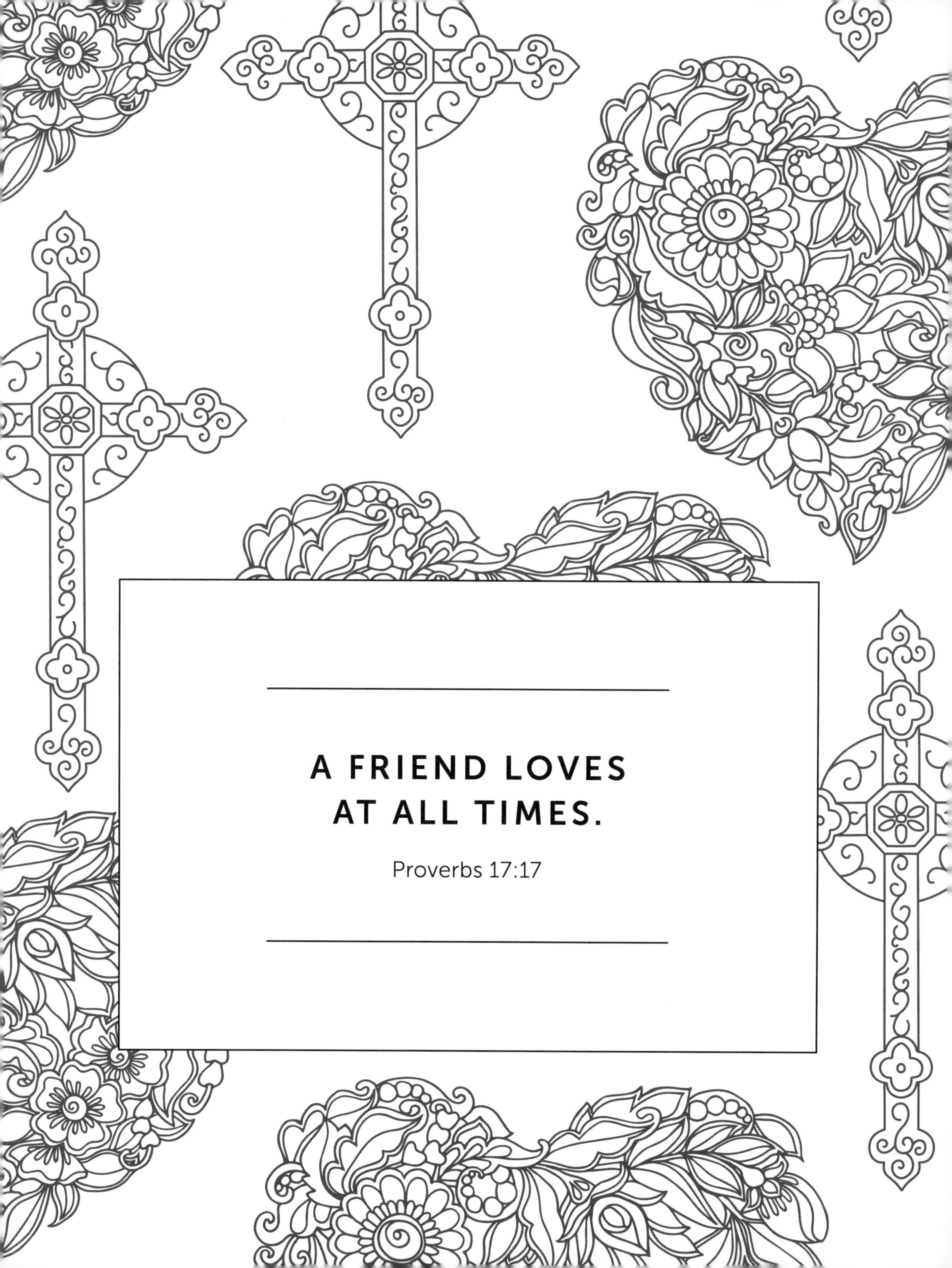
A FRIEND LOVES
AT ALL TIMES.
Proverbs 17:17

Grow
in
Grace

BUT THOSE WHO WAIT
FOR THE LORD WILL RENEW
THEIR STRENGTH.
Isaiah 40:31

WE ARE HIS
BELOVED
FLOCK

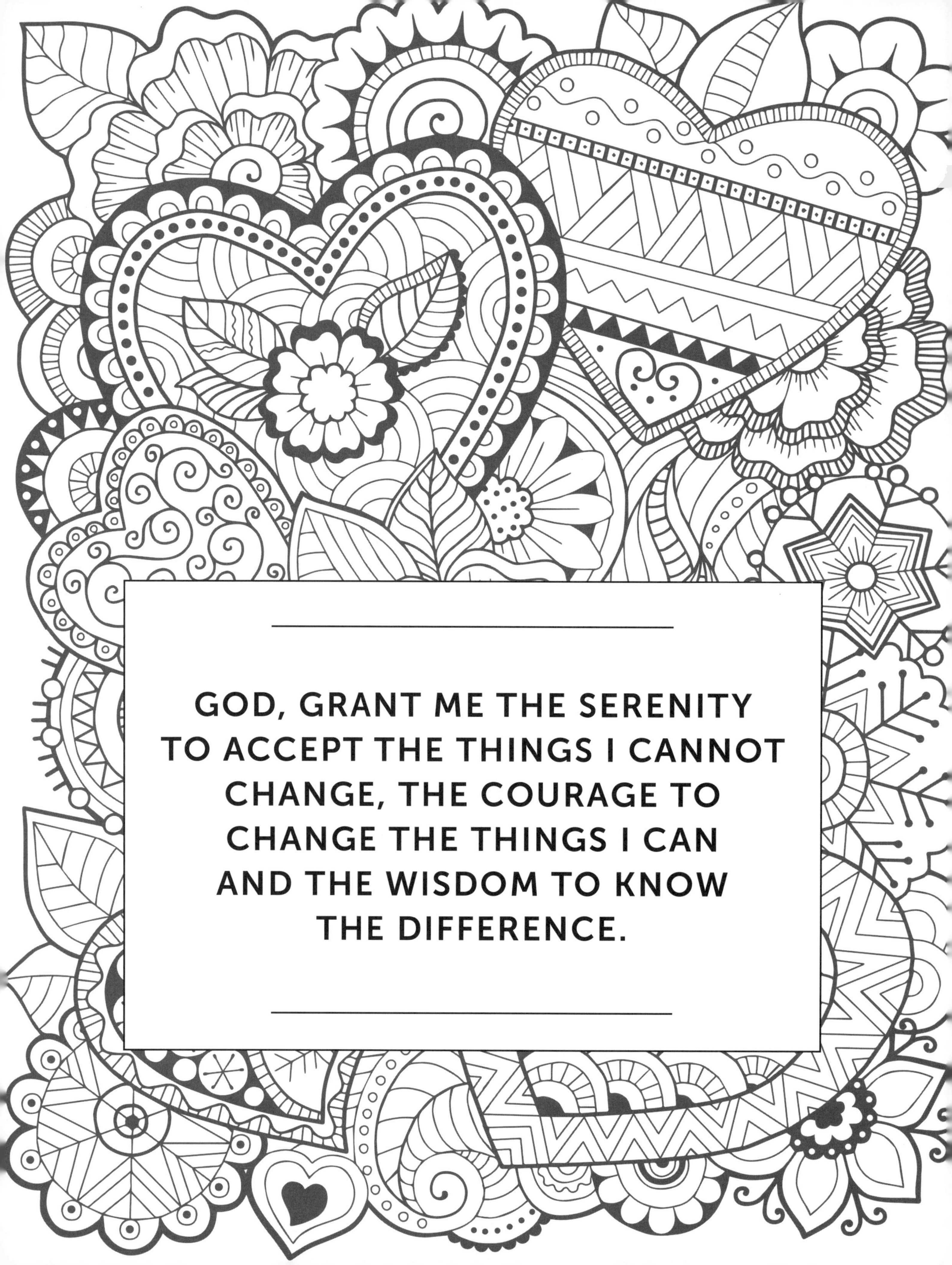
GOD, GRANT ME THE SERENITY
TO ACCEPT THE THINGS I CANNOT
CHANGE, THE COURAGE TO
CHANGE THE THINGS I CAN
AND THE WISDOM TO KNOW
THE DIFFERENCE.

THE
LORD
IS MY
LIGHT

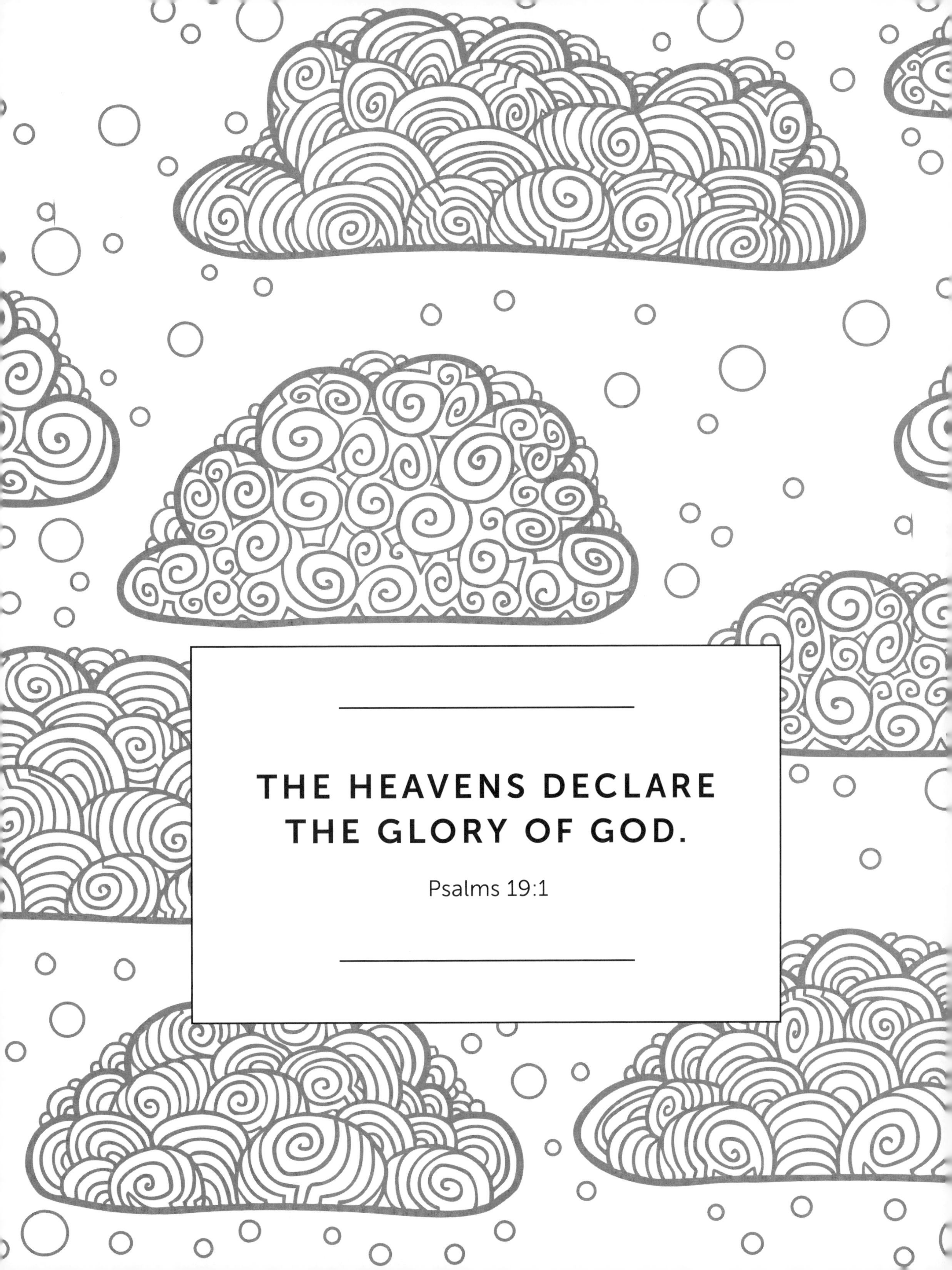
THE HEAVENS DECLARE
THE GLORY OF GOD.
Psalms 19:1

LOVE IS PATIENT
AND IS KIND.
1 Corinthians 13:4

Go
in
peace

I AM LIKE A GREEN OLIVE TREE
IN GOD'S HOUSE. I TRUST
IN GOD'S LOVING KINDNESS
FOREVER AND EVER.
Psalms 52:8

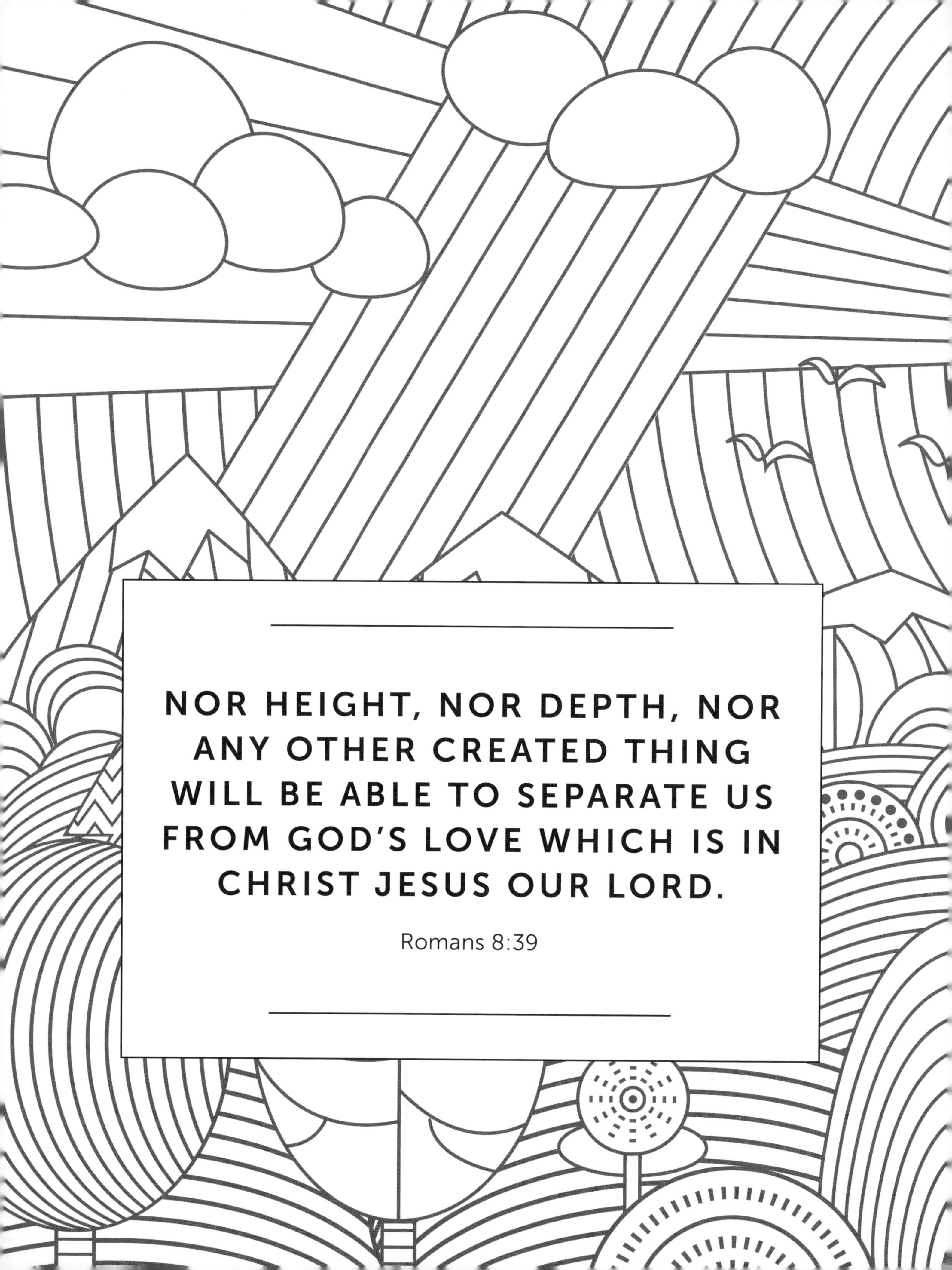
NOR HEIGHT, NOR DEPTH, NOR
ANY OTHER CREATED THING
WILL BE ABLE TO SEPARATE US
FROM GOD'S LOVE WHICH IS IN
CHRIST JESUS OUR LORD.
Romans 8:39

Cherish
His
Word

WATCH! STAND FIRM
IN THE FAITH!
BE COURAGEOUS!
BE STRONG!

1 Corinthians 16:13

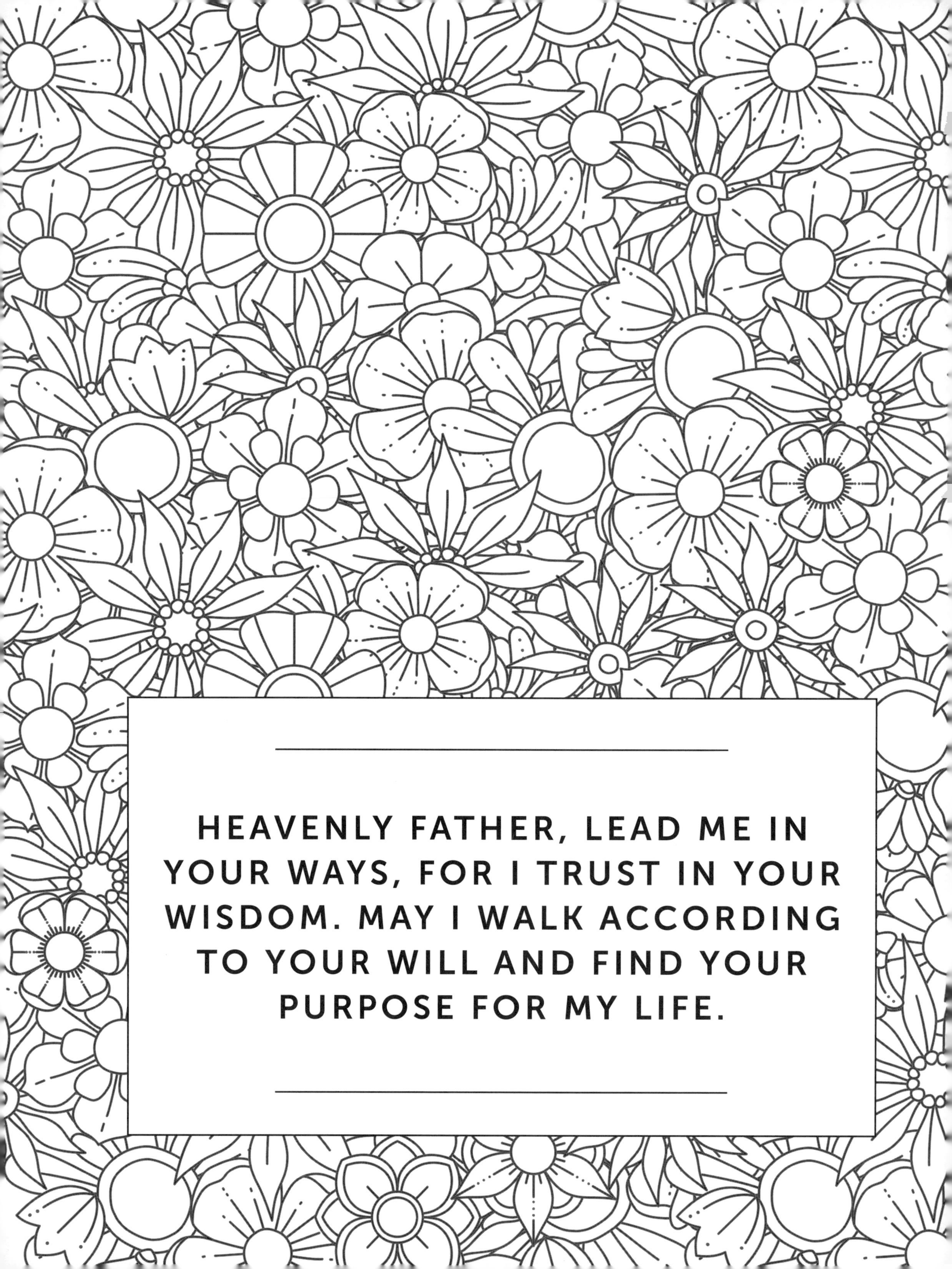
HEAVENLY FATHER, LEAD ME IN YOUR WAYS, FOR I TRUST IN YOUR WISDOM. MAY I WALK ACCORDING TO YOUR WILL AND FIND YOUR PURPOSE FOR MY LIFE.

LEAD
WITH
LOVE

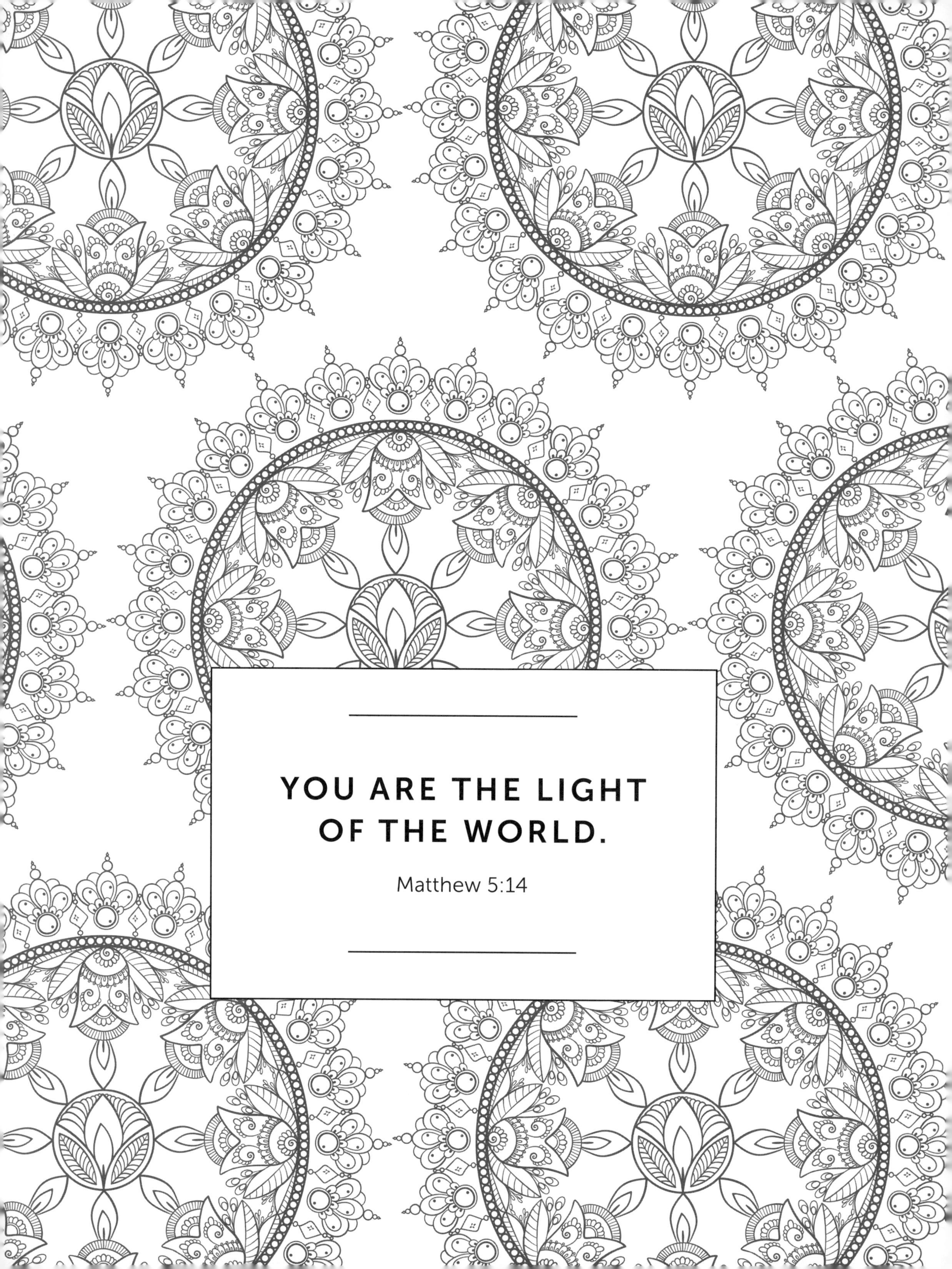
YOU ARE THE LIGHT
OF THE WORLD.
Matthew 5:14

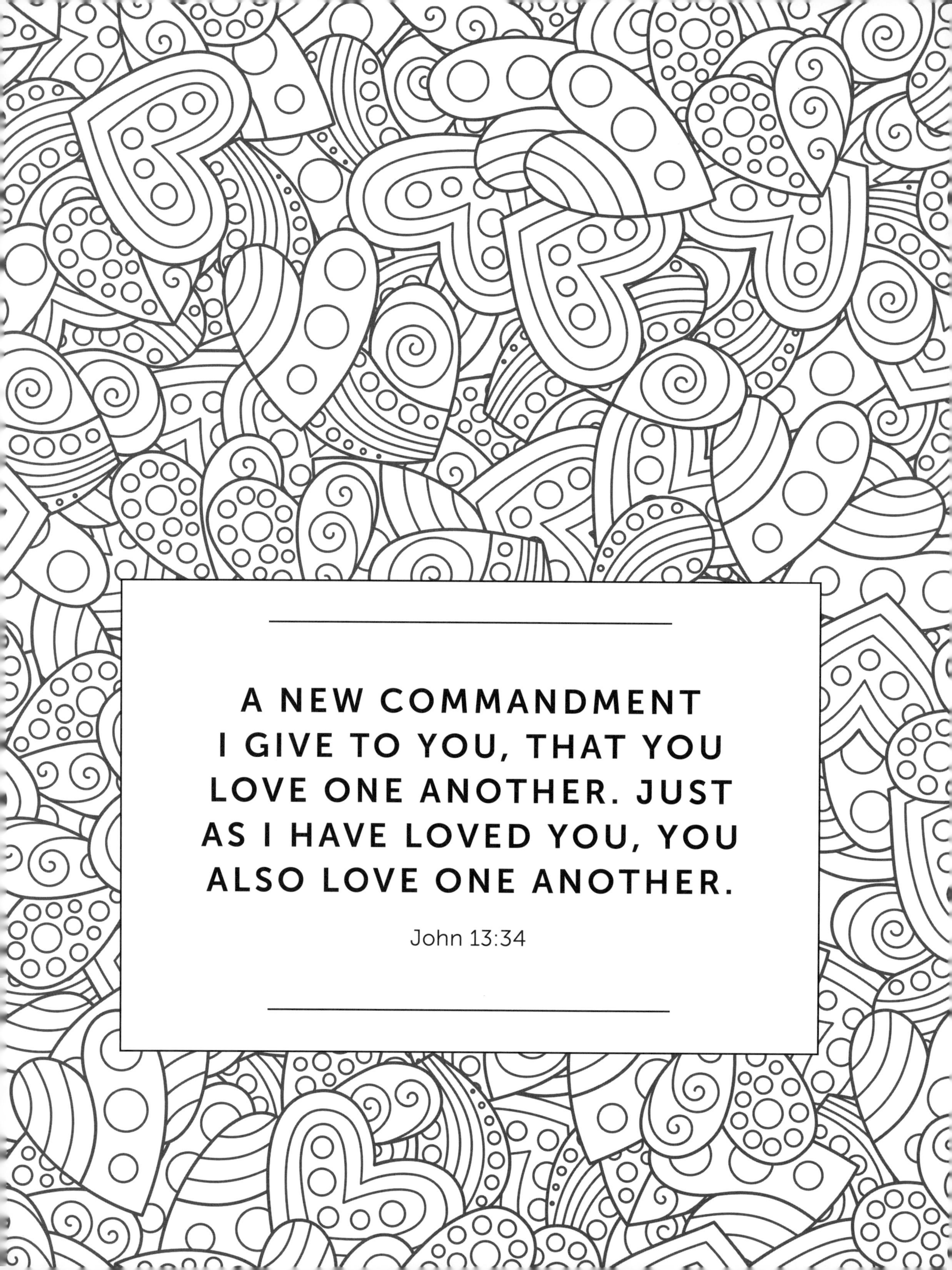
A NEW COMMANDMENT
I GIVE TO YOU, THAT YOU
LOVE ONE ANOTHER. JUST
AS I HAVE LOVED YOU, YOU
ALSO LOVE ONE ANOTHER.
John 13:34

Find
peace

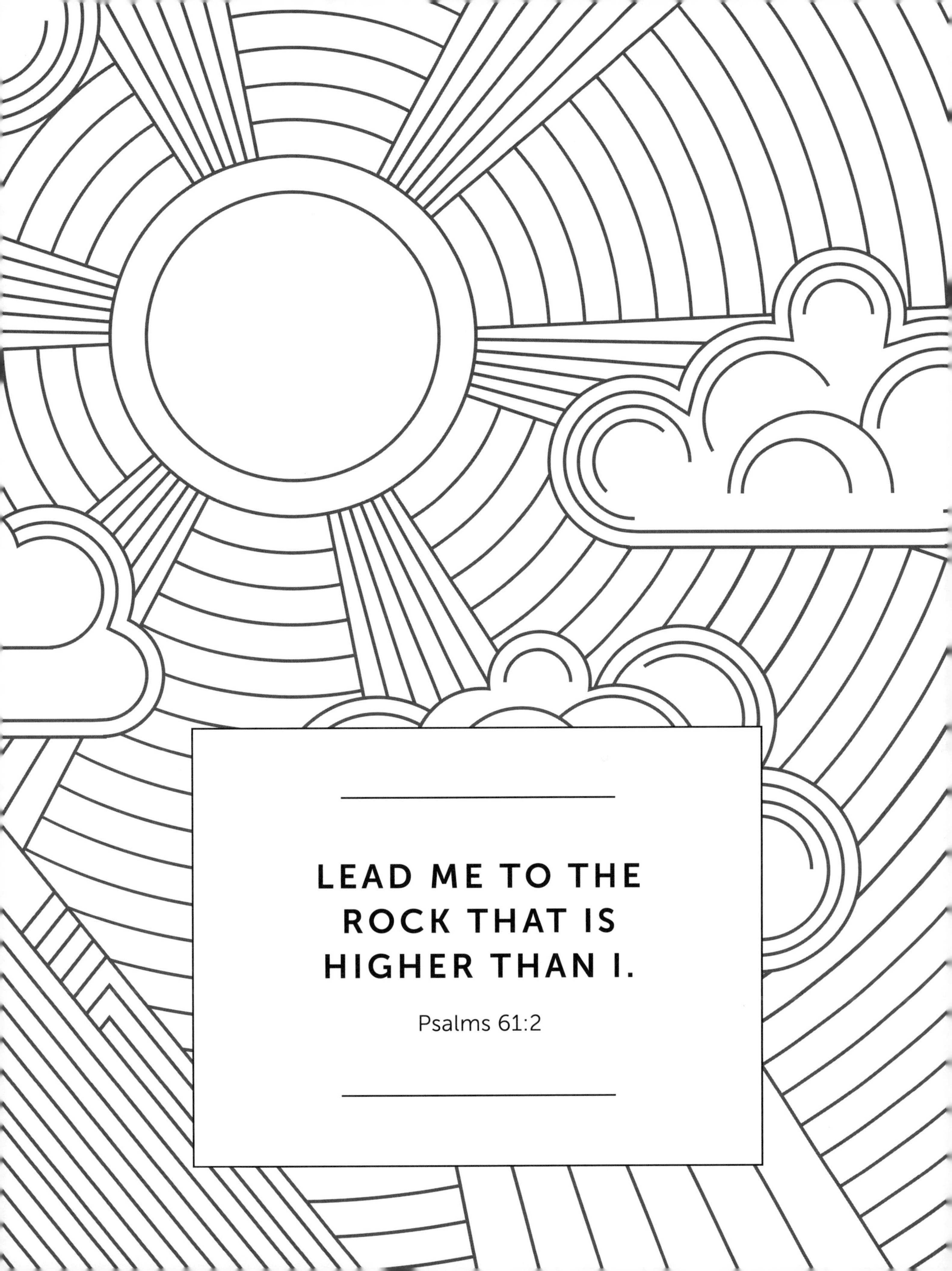
LEAD ME TO THE
ROCK THAT IS
HIGHER THAN I.
Psalms 61:2

BUT NOW FAITH, HOPE AND
LOVE REMAIN – THESE THREE.
THE GREATEST OF THESE
IS LOVE.
1 Corinthians 13:13

Faith is
strength

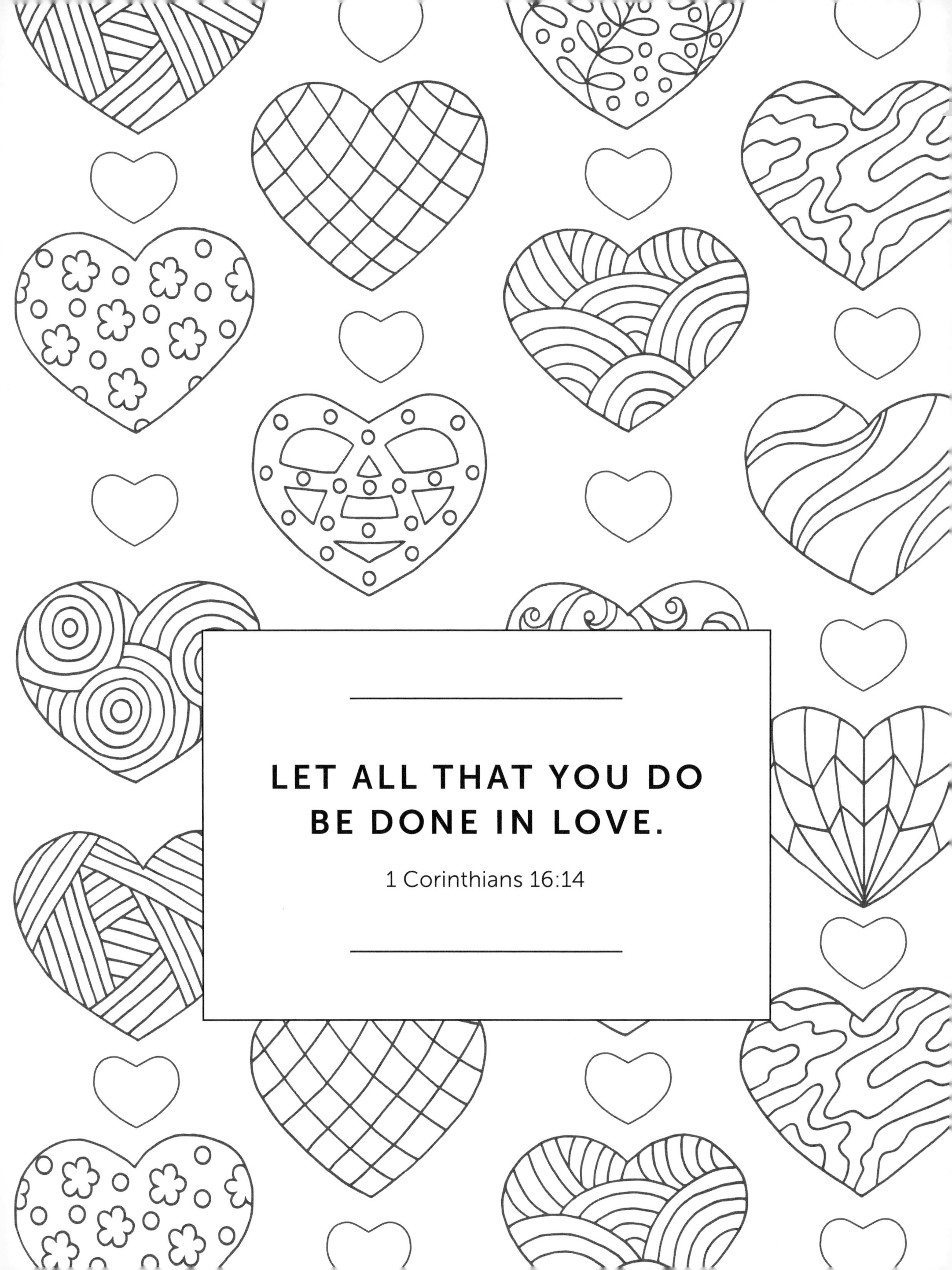
LET ALL THAT YOU DO
BE DONE IN LOVE.
1 Corinthians 16:14

DEAR LORD, AS I BEGIN
THIS DAY, I OFFER IT TO YOU.
GUIDE MY STEPS, FILL ME
WITH YOUR LOVE AND HELP
ME SHINE YOUR LIGHT IN
THE WORLD.

God is good

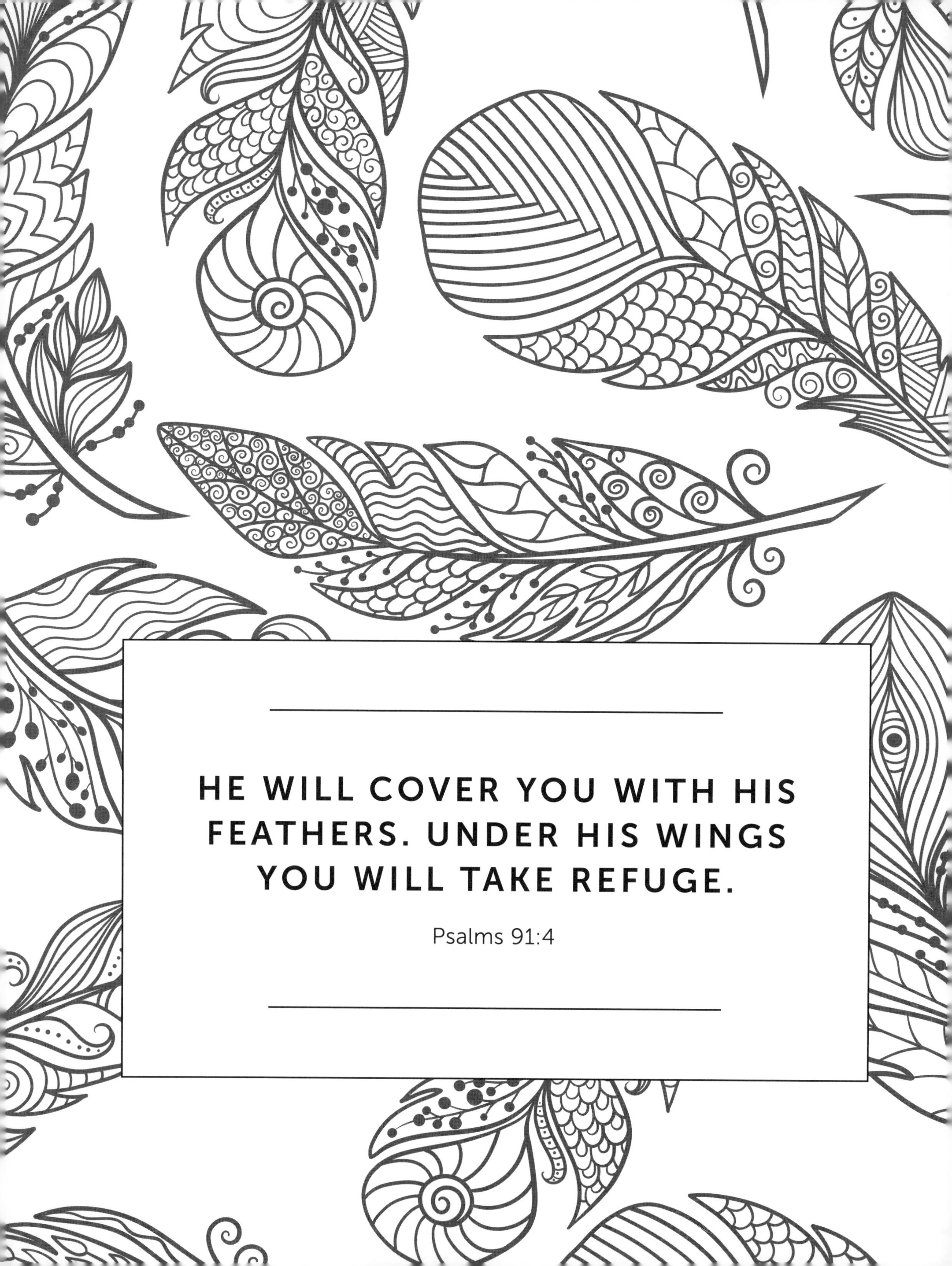
HE WILL COVER YOU WITH HIS FEATHERS. UNDER HIS WINGS YOU WILL TAKE REFUGE.
Psalms 91:4

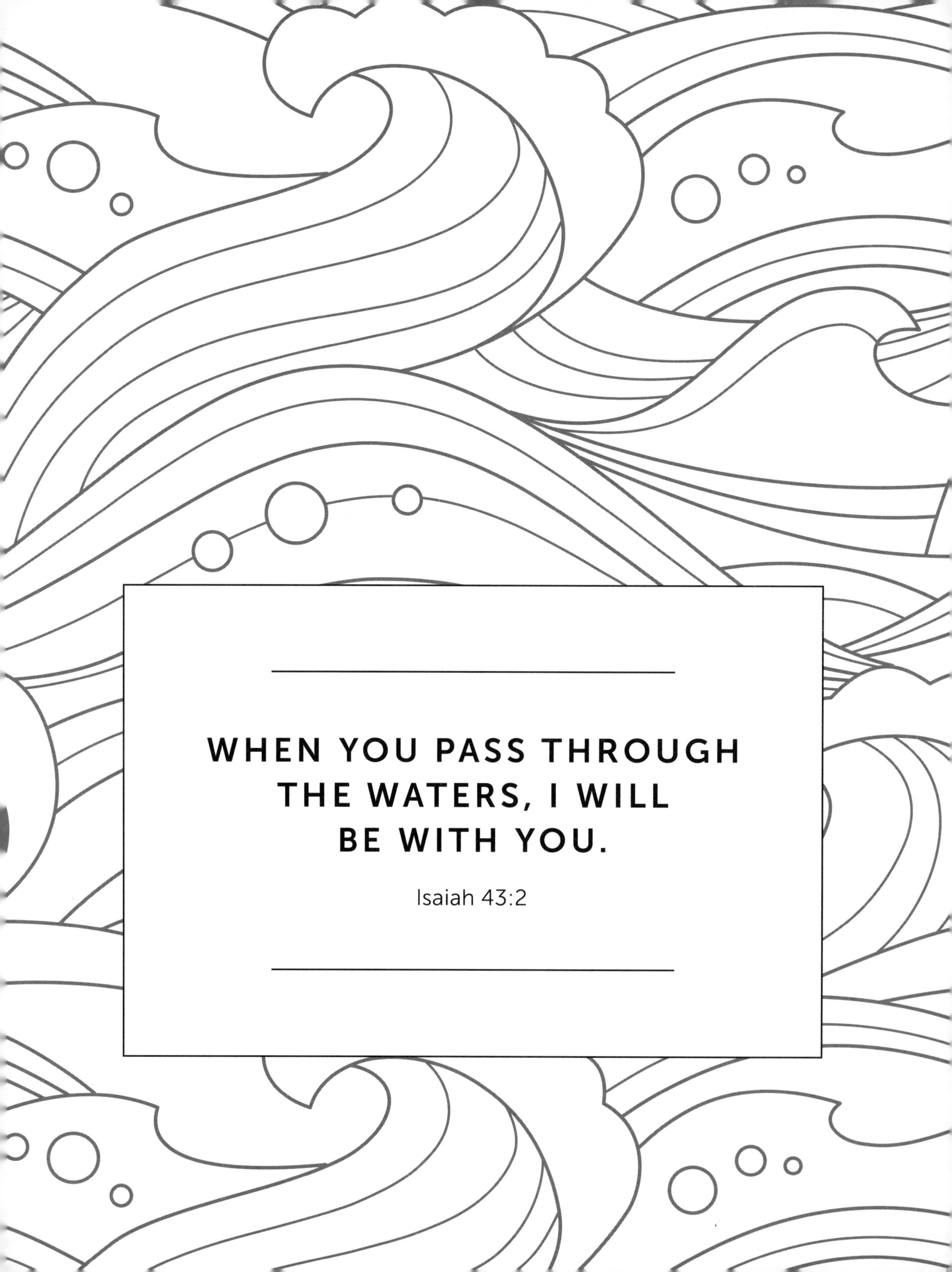
WHEN YOU PASS THROUGH
THE WATERS, I WILL
BE WITH YOU.
Isaiah 43:2

PRAY
EVERY
DAY

HATRED STIRS UP
STRIFE, BUT LOVE
COVERS ALL WRONGS.
Proverbs 10:12

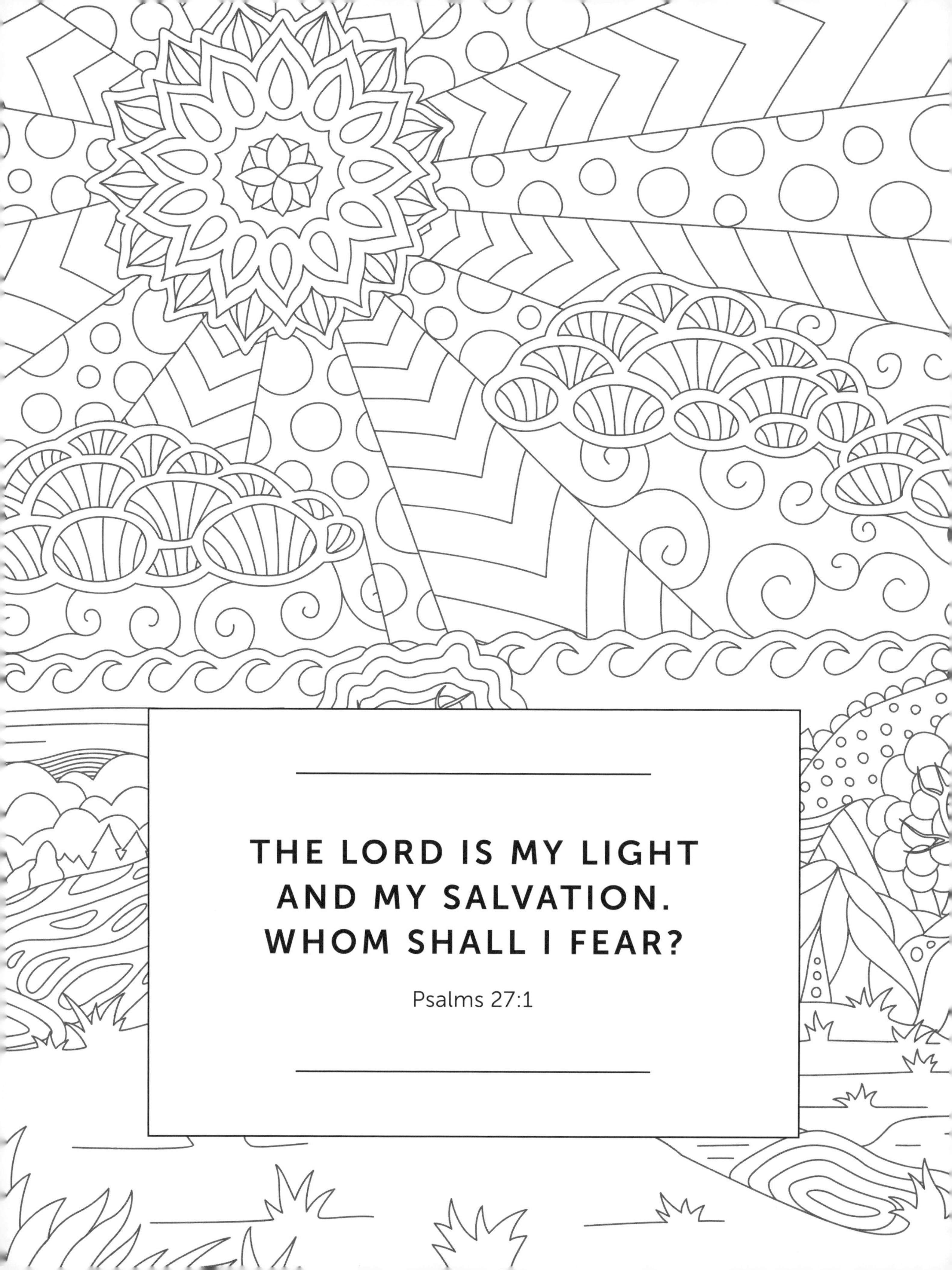
THE LORD IS MY LIGHT
AND MY SALVATION.
WHOM SHALL I FEAR?
Psalms 27:1

THANKS
BE TO
GOD

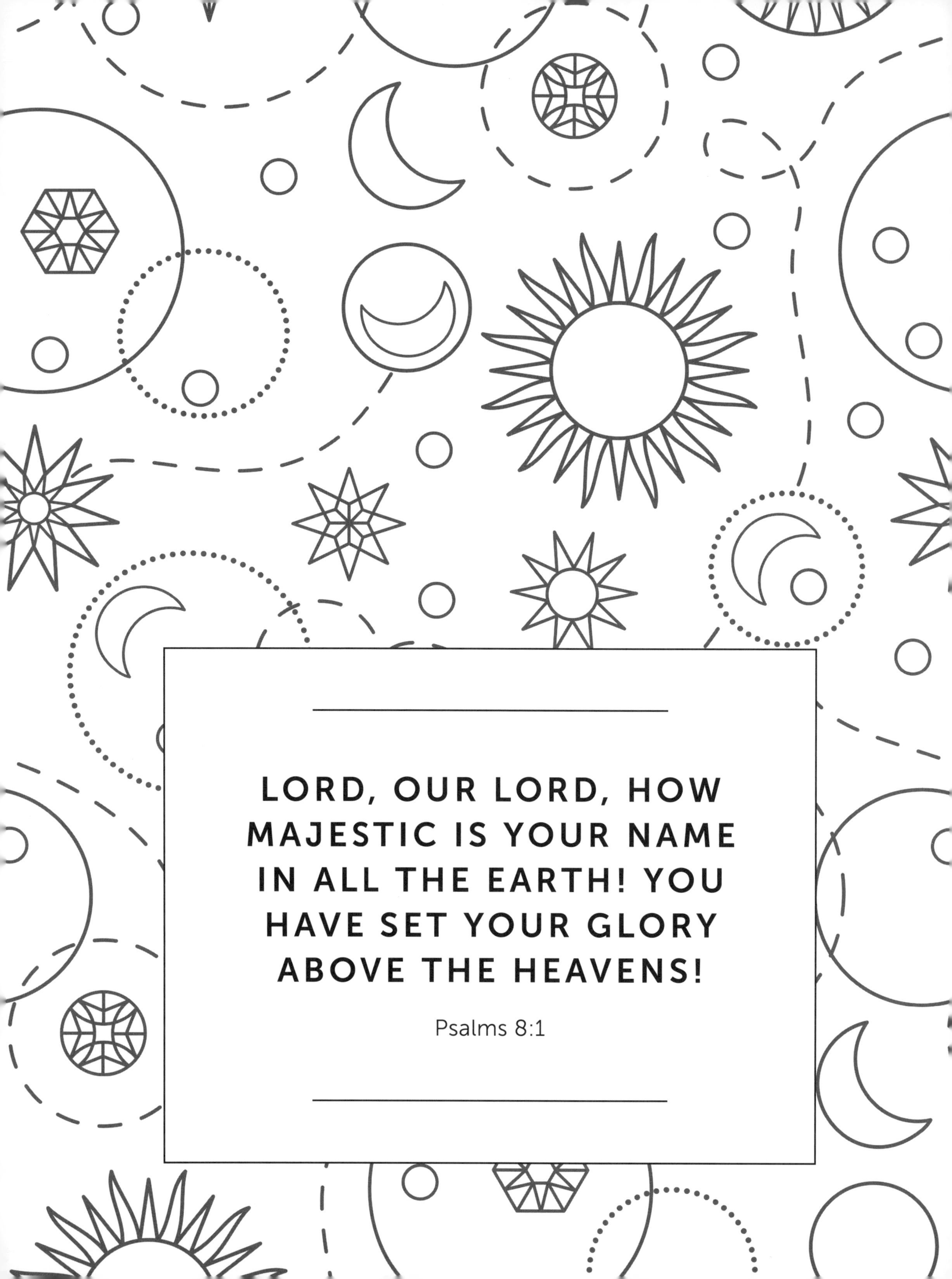
LORD, OUR LORD, HOW MAJESTIC IS YOUR NAME IN ALL THE EARTH! YOU HAVE SET YOUR GLORY ABOVE THE HEAVENS!
Psalms 8:1

GOD, BRING TRANQUILITY
TO MY HEART AND TO THE
TROUBLED PLACES OF
THE WORLD. LET YOUR
PEACE REIGN.

LOVE
YOUR
NEIGHBOR

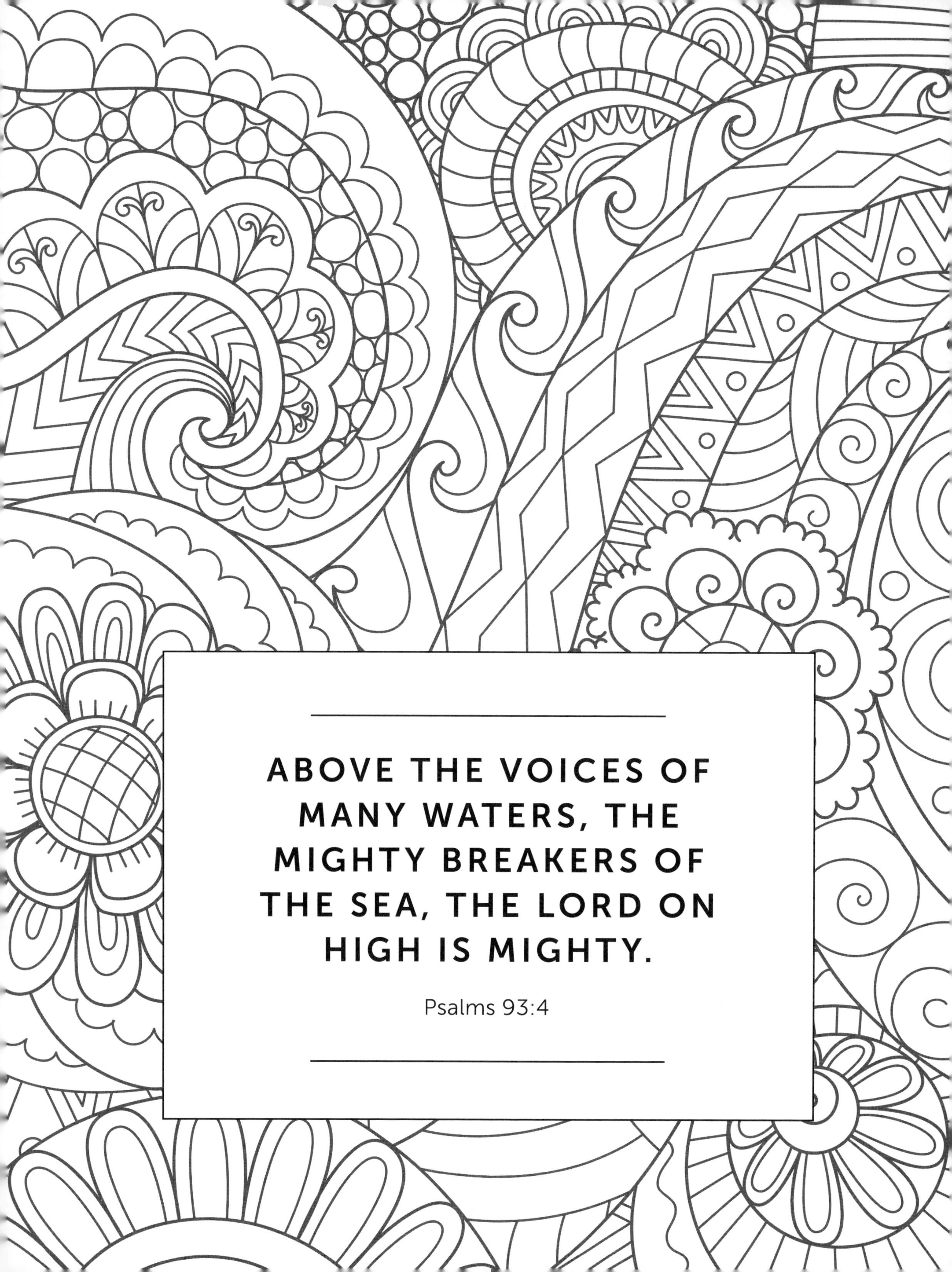
ABOVE THE VOICES OF
MANY WATERS, THE
MIGHTY BREAKERS OF
THE SEA, THE LORD ON
HIGH IS MIGHTY.
Psalms 93:4

SMILE
AND
PRAY

YOU ARE ALL BEAUTIFUL, MY LOVE. THERE IS NO SPOT IN YOU.

Song of Solomon 4:7

REJOICE
in the
BEAUTY
of
CREATION

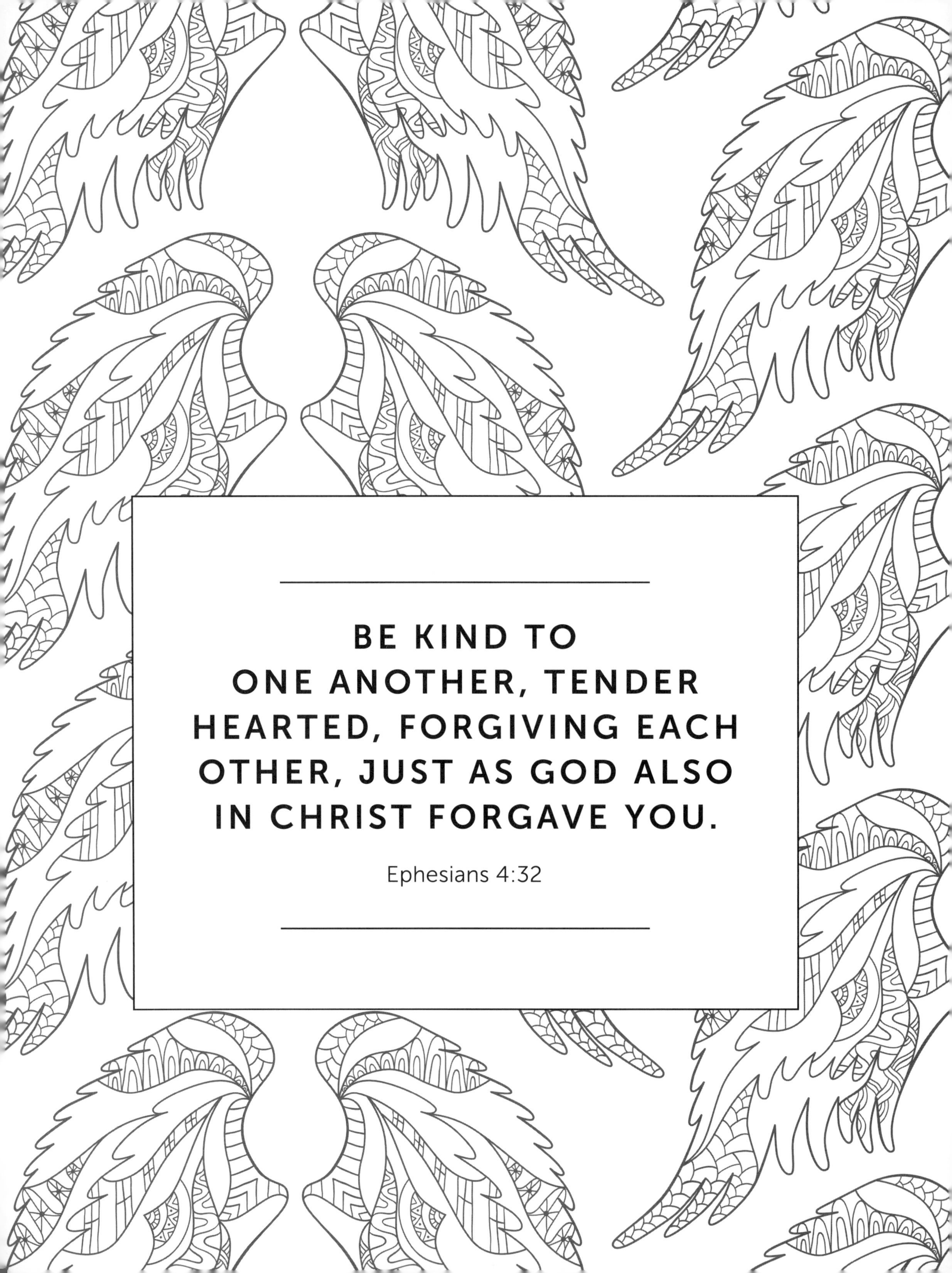
BE KIND TO
ONE ANOTHER, TENDER
HEARTED, FORGIVING EACH
OTHER, JUST AS GOD ALSO
IN CHRIST FORGAVE YOU.
Ephesians 4:32

LET YOUR
FAITH BE
BIGGER THAN
YOUR FEARS

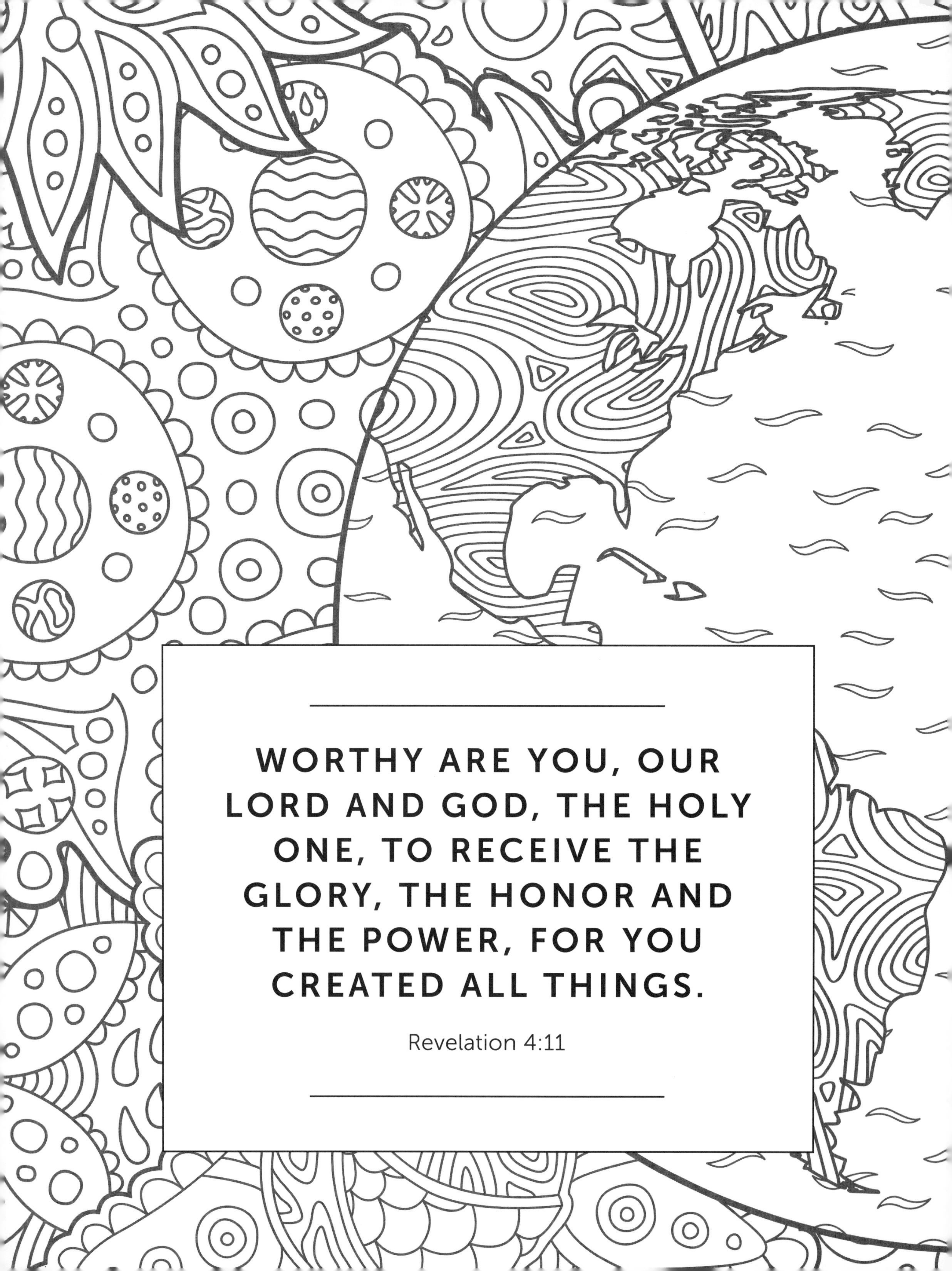
WORTHY ARE YOU, OUR LORD AND GOD, THE HOLY ONE, TO RECEIVE THE GLORY, THE HONOR AND THE POWER, FOR YOU CREATED ALL THINGS.
Revelation 4:11

Dream
of
Heaven

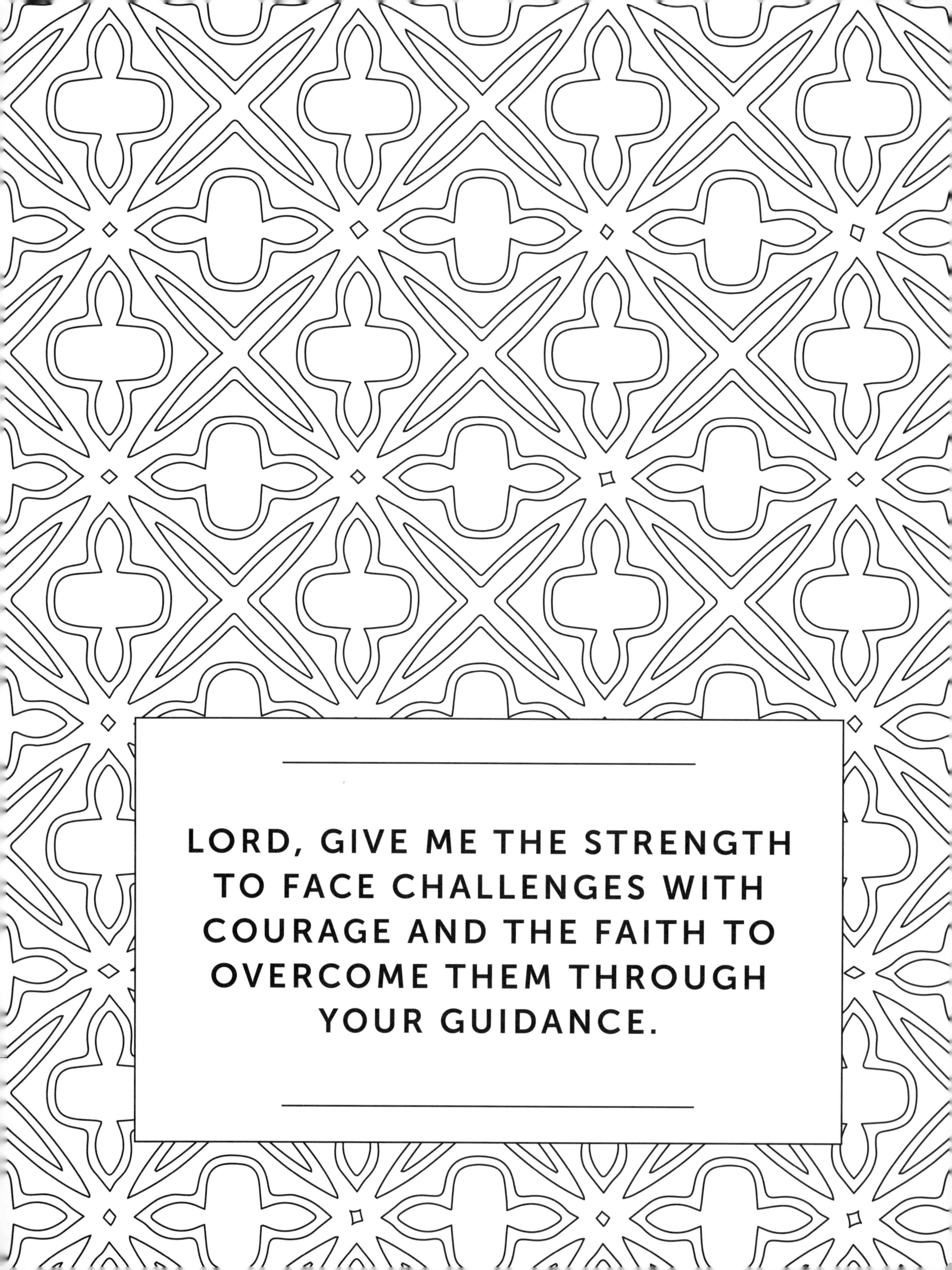
LORD, GIVE ME THE STRENGTH
TO FACE CHALLENGES WITH
COURAGE AND THE FAITH TO
OVERCOME THEM THROUGH
YOUR GUIDANCE.

Jesus
loves
you

THE GRATITUDE COLORING BOOK

A Joyful Journey of Color and Creativity

Paperback
ISBN: 978-1-83799-618-6

This book will take you on a journey of reflection, manifestation and creative expression. Color intricate patterns, contemplate thoughtful quotes and be guided by supportive tips as you uncover everything you have to be grateful for in your life. It's time to take your first step toward becoming a more grateful you.

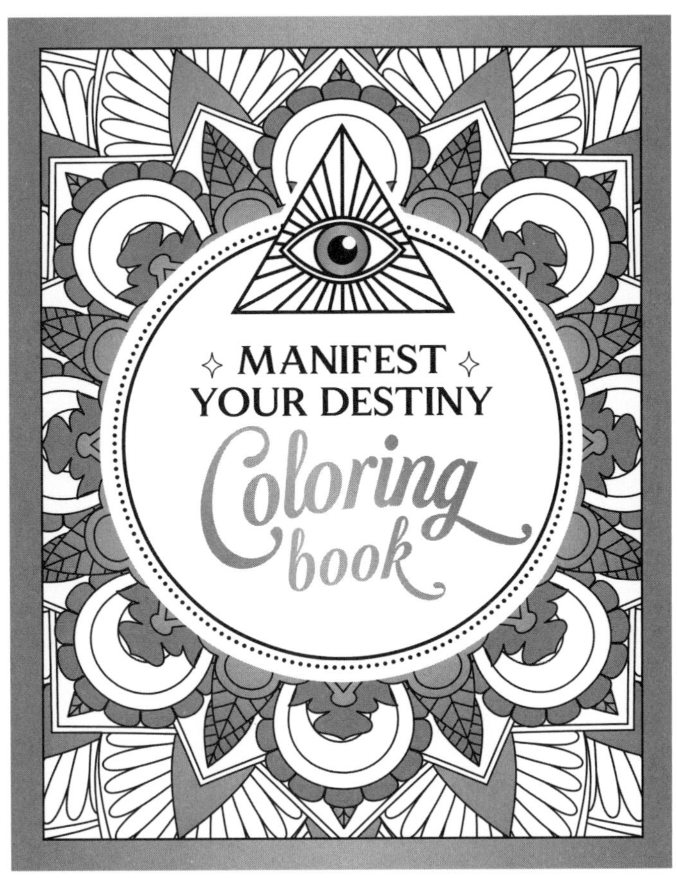

MANIFEST YOUR DESTINY COLORING BOOK

A Mesmerizing Journey of Color and Creativity

Paperback
ISBN: 978-1-83799-100-6

Color in your very own collection of masterpieces and discover the secret to manifesting your dreams with these pages, full of enchanting images and helpful guidance. These intricate patterns will help boost your creativity, raise your vibrations and ultimately support you on your manifesting journey. So relax, and let the universe guide you.

Have you enjoyed this book? If so, find us on Facebook at **Summersdale Publishers**, on Twitter/X at **@Summersdale** and on Instagram and TikTok at **@summersdalebooks** and get in touch. We'd love to hear from you!

www.summersdale.com

IMAGE CREDITS

Cover and p.1 – plant life © ComPix/Shutterstock.com; cover and p.1 – hands © Oleksandr Drypsiak/Shutterstock.com; cover and p.1 – hearts © Yuliya Lins/Shutterstock.com; cover and p.1 – doves © In Art/Shutterstock.com; p.3 and throughout – square crosses © Cernecka Natalja/Shutterstock.com; p.3 – cross and embellishments – abbydesign/Shutterstock.com; p.3 – border © Chorna_black/Shutterstock.com; pp.4–5 – waves © irmairma/Shutterstock.com; pp.6, 54 – corn and lettering © Vera Vin/Shutterstock.com; p.7 – stained-glass window © Cernecka Natalja/Shutterstock.com; p.7 – leaves © Vera Vin/Shutterstock.com; pp.8–9 – plant hearts © Helen Lane/Shutterstock.com; pp.8–9 – cross © MariMuz/Shutterstock.com; p.10 – flowers © Ramunas M/Shutterstock.com; pp.10–11 – tree © SomjaiKing/Shutterstock.com; pp.12–13 – doves © renikca/Shutterstock.com; pp.14–15 – rosettes © Kniazeff/Shutterstock.com; p.15 – Jesus and lamb © Big Boy/Shutterstock.com; pp.16–17 – hearts and flowers © Toporovska Nataliia/Shutterstock.com; p.18 – suns © NATALIA LYUBOVA/Shutterstock.com; p.19 – sun and sea © Christina Designs/Shutterstock.com; pp.20–21 – clouds © natsa/Shutterstock.com; pp.22–23 – cross pattern © Taxiro/Shutterstock.com; pp.24–25 – Christian icons © song_mi/Shutterstock.com; p.25 – stained-glass window © Cernecka Natalja/Shutterstock.com; pp.26–27 – tree © oksanka007/Shutterstock.com; pp.28–29 – landscape © Shpadaruk Aleksei/Shutterstock.com; p.30 – Christian icons © chrupka/Shutterstock.com; p.31 – castle © Cernecka Natalja/Shutterstock.com; pp.32–33 – mountain © H Art/Shutterstock.com; pp.34–35 – flower circle © SkyeCreativeStudio/Shutterstock.com; p.35 – praying woman © maritel/Shutterstock.com; pp.36–37 – hearts © mis-Tery/Shutterstock.com; pp.36–37 – tree and fans © SomjaiKing/Shutterstock.com; pp.38–39 – candles pattern © SoulPhotos/Shutterstock.com; pp.40–41 – pattern © Nata__Smilyk/Shutterstock.com; p.42 – flowers frame © ComPix/Shutterstock.com; pp.42–43 – Christian icons © chrupka/Shutterstock.com; pp.44–45 – mountain landscape © Shpadaruk Aleksei/Shutterstock.com; pp.46–47 – heart of flowers © SomjaiKing/Shutterstock.com; p.48 – cross © Nunushik1/Shutterstock.com; p.49 – Mary and Jesus © AuraArt/Shutterstock.com; p.49 – pattern © Rikley Stock/Shutterstock.com; pp.50–51 – hearts © Shamilini/Shutterstock.com; pp.52–53 – sunshine © ImHope/Shutterstock.com; p.54 – corn, grapes and wafer © chrupka/Shutterstock.com; p.54 – branches © chrupka/Shutterstock.com; p.54 – swirls © abbydesign/Shutterstock.com; p.55 – stained-glass flowers © Lexver/Shutterstock.com; pp.56–57 – feathers © Shamilini/Shutterstock.com; pp.58–59 – waves © irmairma/Shutterstock.com; p.60 – flower frame © nichy/Shutterstock.com; pp.60–61 – praying hands and flowers © maritel/Shutterstock.com; pp.62–63 – doves, heart and leaves © Kaewta/Shutterstock.com; pp.62–63 – cross © Nunushik1/Shutterstock.com; pp.64–65 – landscape © Rikley Stock/Shutterstock.com; p.66 – olives © Alex Korolchuk/Shutterstock.com; p.66 – grapes © Gray Cat/Shutterstock.com; p.67 – church © Zagory/Shutterstock.com; pp.68–69 – sun, moon and stars pattern © AuraArt/Shutterstock.com; pp.70–71 – dove © arawizrd/Shutterstock.com; pp.72–73 – plant heart © ComPix/Shutterstock.com; pp.72–73 – flowers and leaves © Eva Kali/Shutterstock.com; pp.74–75 – waves © SomjaiKing/Shutterstock.com; p.76 – pattern © MOCHALOV GENNADII/Shutterstock.com; p.77 – sun © Tanya Leanovich/Shutterstock.com; pp.78–79 – abstract pattern © Olena Kryvoruchko/Shutterstock.com; p.80 – Christian icons © Noch/Shutterstock.com; p.81 – arches © Labetskiy Alexandr/Shutterstock.com; pp.82–83 – wings © Tanya Leanovich/Shutterstock.com; p.84 – faith statement © mdrakibul1n1a76/Shutterstock.com; p.85 – bread and wine © abbydesign/Shutterstock.com; pp.86–87 – earth © Rikley Stock/Shutterstock.com; pp.88–89 – cross and clouds © Zagory/Shutterstock.com; pp.90–91 – geometric pattern © Joe_Biden/Shutterstock.com; p.92 – cross © Nunushik1/Shutterstock.com; p.92 – heart © Yuliya Lins/Shutterstock.com; p.93 – cross © abbydesign/Shutterstock.com; p.93 – fields © Lybava/Shutterstock.com